NATIONAL GEOGRAPHIC
KiDS

SHARKS
STICKER ACTIVITY
BOOK

Pull out the sticker sheets and keep
them by you as you complete each page.
There are also lots of extra stickers to
use in this book or anywhere you want!
Have fun!

NATIONAL GEOGRAPHIC
Washington, D.C.

Consultant: John Richardson
Editorial, Design, and Production by
make believe ideas

Picture credits: All images Shutterstock unless as follows: **Alamy:** 4 br, 40 bl; **Chris Dascher/iStockphoto:** 5 tm, 9 find-the-difference activity: lemon shark x2, 10 tl, 20 tr; ml, 37 m; **Dreamstime:** 30 tl;
Fotosearch: 7 bm, 15 br, 20 bl; br; **Greg Amptman's Undersea Discoveries:** 1 br (tiger shark), 17 tl; **Island Effects/ iStockphoto:** 1 tr, 18 br, 28 tl; **ITF:** 30 m (blue fish); tm; tr; m; br (clownfish x4), 31 m; bl x2 (clownfish x3);
James R. D. Scott: 12 ml; **Klaas Lingbeek-van Kranen/iStockphoto:** 18 ml; **Make Believe Ideas:** 4 bl (stingray), 9 find-the-difference activity: lobster x2; seahorse x2; sea star x2, 15 bm, 31m (fish); ml (green fish), 37 mr; bm;
Make Believe Ideas/Graham Kennedy: 32 mr, 34 tl, 39 ml; **Maria M. Mudd:** 1 br (tooth), 35 tr; **Mark Doherty:** 20 mr, 22 tl; **Ocean/Corbis:** 17 bl; **Stephen Frink/Getty Images:** 24 tm; **Teguh Tirtaputra:** 15 m; **Willyam Bradberry:** 20 tl.

Sticker pages: All images Shutterstock unless as follows: **Alamy:** 6, 7 great white shark; leopard shark, 12, 13 leopard shark x2; **Chris Dascher/iStockphoto:** great white shark: 2, 3, 4, 5 (parts x5), 22, 23 (x3), 24, 25,
12, 13 lemon shark; **Corbis:** whitetip reef shark: 30, 31, 40; **Fotolia:** 30, 31 sea anemone; **Fotosearch:** 16, 17 squid, 26, 27 blue spotted stingray, 30, 31 squid; **Georgette Douwma:** silky shark: 4, 5, 22, 23 (x2);
Island Effects/iStockphoto: whale shark (front on): 2, 3, 22, 23 (x2), 28, 29; **ITF:** 8, 9 yellow fish x2; orange fish x2; **Jeff Mauritzen/National Geographic:** 36, 37 whitetip reef shark; **Klaas Lingbeek-van Kranen/iStockphoto:**
whale shark: 22, 23, 28, 29; **Make Believe Ideas:** 8, 9 goldfish, 16, 17 fish; hot dog; ice cream, 18, 19 seaweed x2, 24, 25 stingray, 26, 27 beach ball; ice cream, 30, 31 fish x2, 36, 37 blacktip reef shark, 40 crab; fish,
Extra Stickers (Sheet 2) yellow fish x4; orange fish x8; **Make Believe Ideas/The National Marine Aquarium:** 4, 5 ray (ml), 16, 17 sand tiger shark, 24, 25 gray fish x3; **Mark Doherty:** scalloped hammerhead shark: 2, 3, 4, 5, 10, 11,
20, 21, 36, 37; **NaturePL/Dan Burton:** 18, 19 basking shark; **Rich Carey:** 30, 31 reef shark, 40 nurse shark; **Tatiana Belova:** 4, 5 eagle ray (mr); **Willyam Bradberry:** gray reef shark: 20, 21, 22, 23.

Printed in China. 15/MBI/3

Check out these amazing **sharks!**

Sharks have been living on our planet since before the dinosaurs!

Sticker sharks around the planet!

There are more than 450 different types of sharks.

Fill the ocean with swimming sharks!

Make the seaweed colorful!

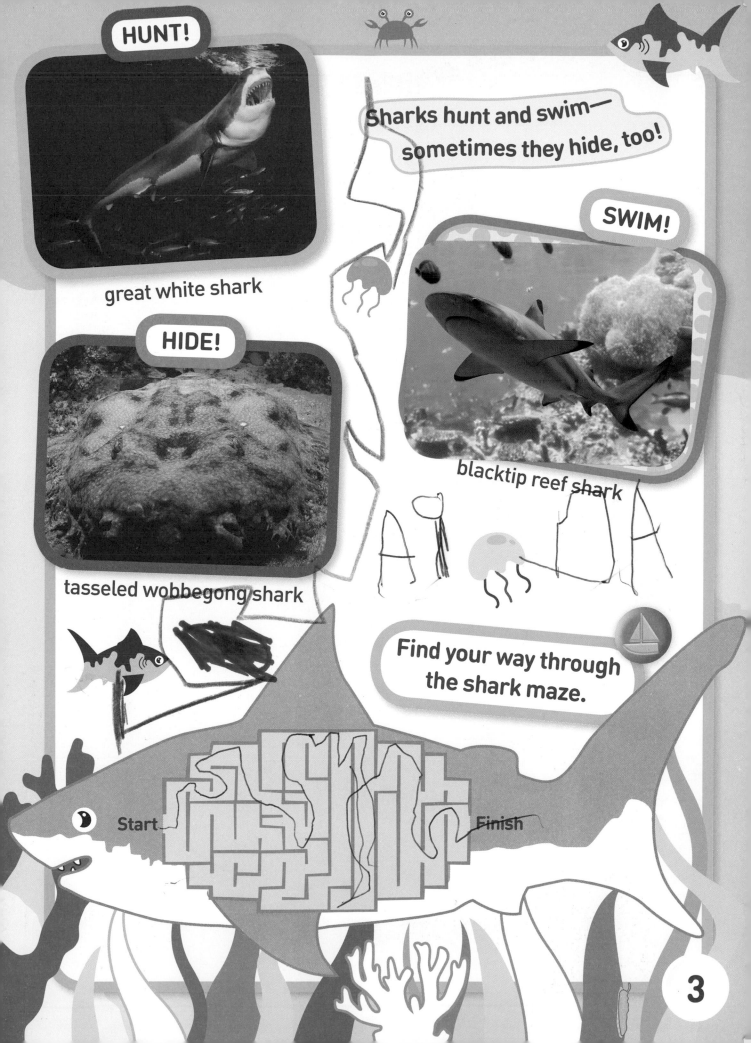

HUNT!

great white shark

Sharks hunt and swim— sometimes they hide, too!

SWIM!

blacktip reef shark

HIDE!

tasseled wobbegong shark

Find your way through the shark maze.

Start

Finish

What is a shark?

A shark's skeleton is made from the same stuff that's inside our noses and ears!

Sticker the shark's skeleton!

RAYS

Rays are related to sharks.

SHARKS

Find the missing stickers to sort the sharks from the rays.

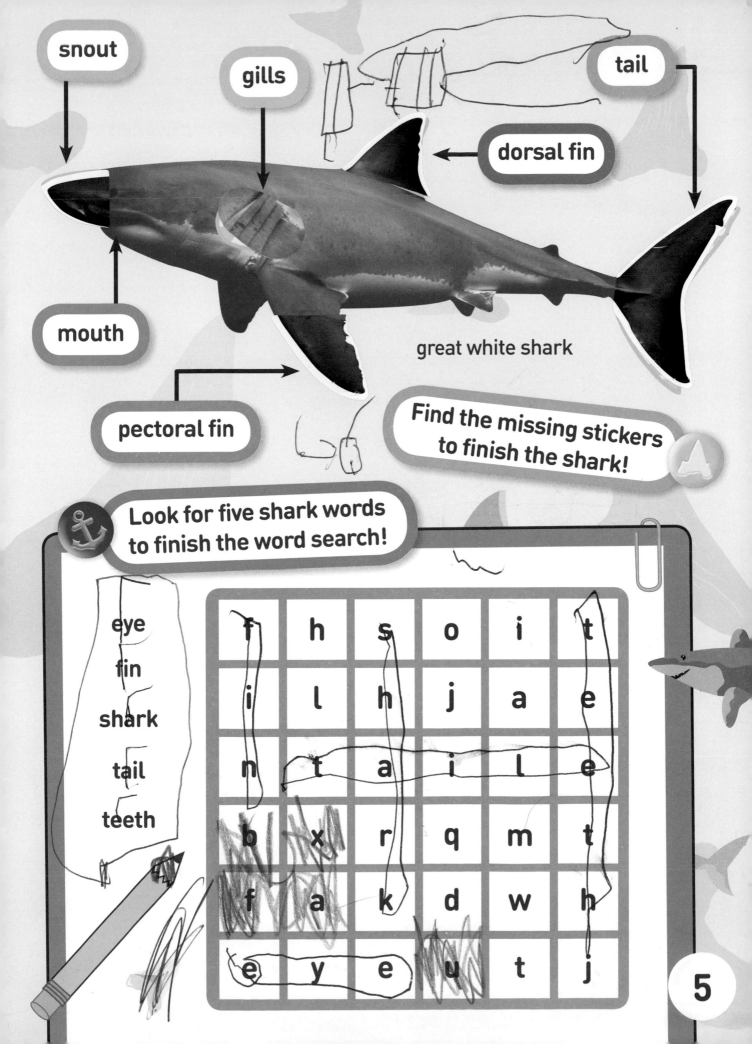

snout

gills

tail

dorsal fin

mouth

great white shark

pectoral fin

Find the missing stickers to finish the shark!

Look for five shark words to finish the word search!

eye
fin
shark
tail
teeth

f	h	s	o	i	t
i	l	h	j	a	e
n	t	a	i	l	e
b	x	r	q	m	t
f	a	k	d	w	h
e	y	e	u	t	j

5

Super swimmers

Follow the trails to find out who swims the fastest!

great white shark

blue shark

Some sharks are speedy swimmers, but most travel at just 1.5 miles an hour (2.5 km/h).

leopard shark

WINNER

Draw a new tail fin for the thresher shark.

1

Thresher sharks have the longest tail fin of any shark! It grows up to a massive 10 feet (3 m) long!

Sticker the missing tails for the busy sharks.

thresher shark

7

Sharks have terrific teeth!

Color and sticker the sharks.

tiny teeth
whale shark

flat, crushing teeth
common smoothhound shark

Sharks' teeth are set in rows. When a tooth falls out, another tooth moves forward to take its place.

pointed teeth
sand tiger shark

Sticker more teeth, then add fun fish to feed the shark!

8

Find eight differences between the underwater scenes.

Sharks have extra senses!

Help the shark sense its prey!

Sharks sense things by sight, smell, sound, touch, taste—and electricity!

lemon shark

Start

Fihish

Draw something smelly for the sharks.

10

Caribbean reef shark

Sticker sounds for the shark to hear.

Sharks have a good sense of hearing and hear deep, low sounds the best.

Some sharks' eyes glow green in the dark!

Sticker the sharks' green eyes!

11

Gills help sharks breathe!

gray reef shark

sand tiger shark

Connect the dots!

gills

bluntnose sixgill shark

Most sharks have five gills, but some have six or seven!

Many sharks must keep swimming at all times in order to breathe.

Follow the trails to help the shark get out of the cave.

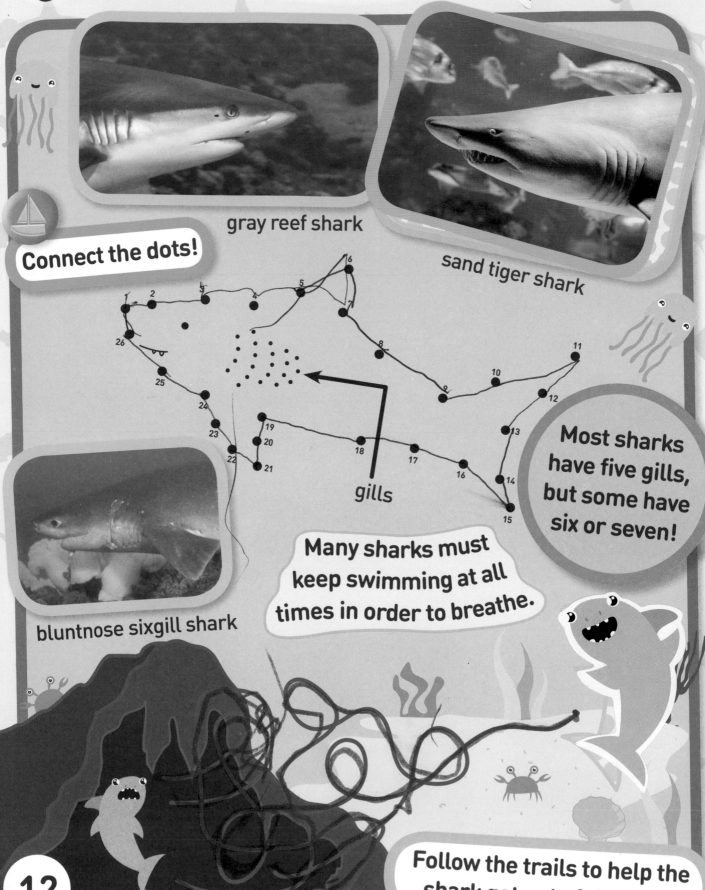

Use the grid to draw the shark!

Nurse sharks pump water over their gills so they can stay still on the seabed for a long time.

Sticker more sharks on the seabed.

leopard shark

13

Sharks can really **blend in!**

Sticker sharks into the correct colors to help them hide!

The color of a shark's skin can help it hide from attackers or sneak up on its prey!

angel shark

Draw and color your own shark pattern!

14

whale shark

tiger shark

Finish the shark patterns.

Find six tiny sharks hiding on the page!

This shark looks like seaweed! Its strange mouth tricks fish into coming near it.

tasseled wobbegong shark

Sticker funny disguises for these sea creatures!

Hunters of the sea

Sharks are predators. A predator is an animal that hunts other animals.

sand tiger shark

Caribbean reef sharks

A Draw and sticker a meal for the sharks.

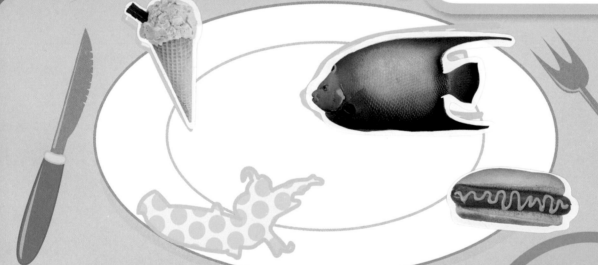

Most sharks don't chew their food; they swallow it whole or in large chunks!

whitetip reef sharks

lemon shark

Tiger sharks have a really mixed diet! As well as fish, they hunt animals such as seabirds, dolphins, sea snakes, seals, and sea turtles.

Sticker fun food for the tiger shark!

Find the dinner that's different.

Some sharks are gentle giants!

whale shark

basking shark

Filter-feeding sharks have massive mouths, but they only eat tiny plants and animals.

Sticker more remoras.

Remoras are fish that attach to large sea animals to hitch a ride and feed on leftover food!

Follow the trails to find the fishy shake!

Every few hours, basking sharks swallow enough water to fill an Olympic-size swimming pool!

Color and sticker to create a giant drink for the basking shark!

19

Baby sharks are called **pups!**

Find the missing stickers, then draw lines to match each pup to its mom!

gray reef shark

great white shark

scalloped hammerhead shark

Draw your own shark pup!

Some sharks lay spiral-shaped eggs! To keep the eggs safe, the sharks hide them between rocks.

Color the mermaid's purse.

shark egg

An empty shark egg is called a mermaid's purse!

How many mermaid's purses can you find?

_____

zebra shark

Sticker more eggs and color the coral!

Sharks are on the move!

Sticker sharks on a long-distance race!

A great white shark named Nicole swam from South Africa to Australia and back, in just nine months!

Sticker the winning shark!

FINISH

2 1 3

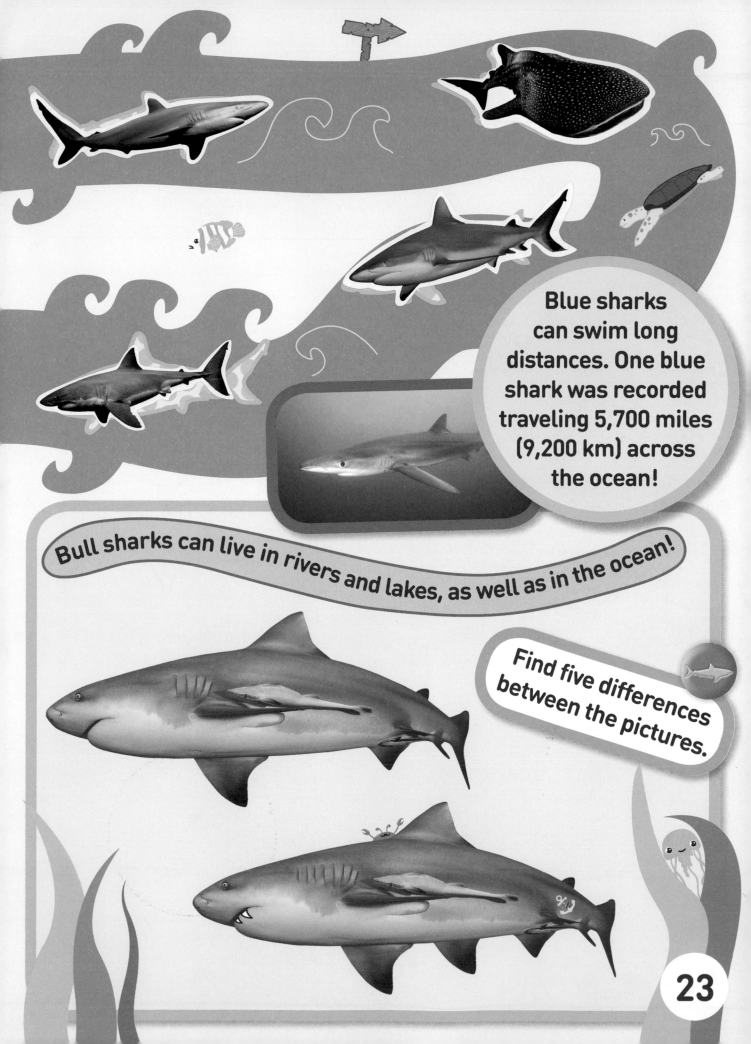

Blue sharks can swim long distances. One blue shark was recorded traveling 5,700 miles (9,200 km) across the ocean!

Bull sharks can live in rivers and lakes, as well as in the ocean!

Find five differences between the pictures.

Incredible great white sharks

Great white sharks have more than 250 sharp teeth!

Color the shark teeth!

Great whites hunt fish, dolphins, seals, sea lions, and even some whales!

Sticker the missing sea creatures.

When hunting, great whites can launch themselves out of the water!

Great whites take their name from their white bellies!

Count the sharks and then find the one that's different.

How many sharks can you count? ....

25

Hammerhead sharks have **amazing** heads!

Connect the dots and find the missing stickers to finish the hammerhead!

A weird-shaped head actually gives the hammerhead a better sense of smell. This helps the shark hunt its prey.

scalloped hammerhead shark

spotted eagle ray

Hammerheads love eating stingrays!

Whale sharks are enormous!

The whale shark is the largest fish in the world! It can grow to be as long as a school bus!

Color and sticker the trophy!

Sticker the sharks and then circle the one that is longer in each pair.

Whale sharks' spotted patterns are unique—just like fingerprints are for each of us.

Sticker more spots on the whale shark!

Draw colorful spots on this whale shark!

Create your own pattern for this whale shark!

29

Exploring the coral reefs!

Find the missing stickers to fill the reef!

Many sharks live in and around coral reefs, including blacktip reef sharks and Caribbean reef sharks.

Be a reef explorer! How many different sea creatures can you count?

....

sea star

lobster

Color the shark.

Color the coral reef.

clownfish

.... seahorse

31

World's **weirdest** sharks!

Some sharks do not look like sharks at all!

Find the missing shark, then decorate the picture frames!

The unusual goblin shark is a pinkish-white color!

Color the goblin shark.

The cookie-cutter shark bites cookie-shaped chunks out of its prey!

Sticker a spot for the epaulette shark.

32

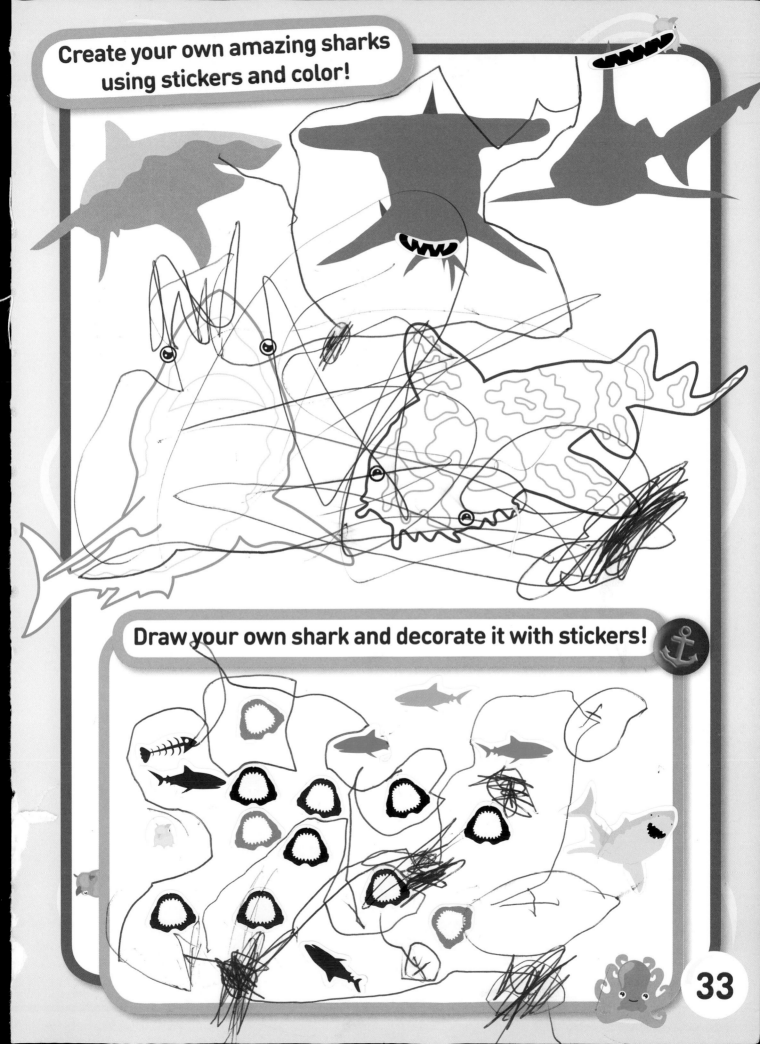

Create your own amazing sharks using stickers and color!

Draw your own shark and decorate it with stickers!

33

Megalodon was an ancient shark!

Megalodon lived millions of years ago. At about 50 feet (15 m) long, it is thought to be the biggest shark ever!

Sticker a diver to find out how big megalodon was!

Help the diver find the shark tooth and then get back to the boat.

Start

Finish

Megalodon means "big tooth." This shark's teeth were as big as a human hand!

Draw and color more teeth for megalodon!

Find the seven megalodon teeth!

Find the missing stickers to finish the patterns.

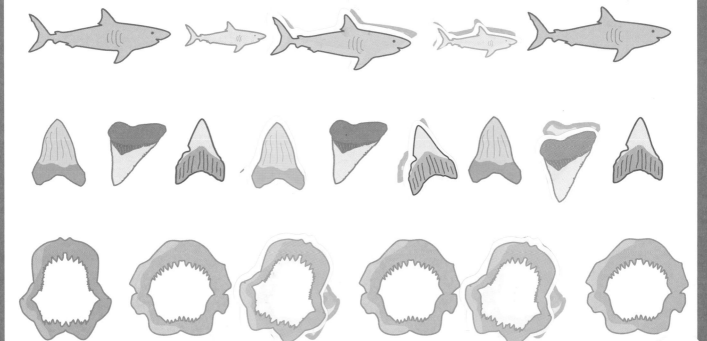

Be a shark Scientist!

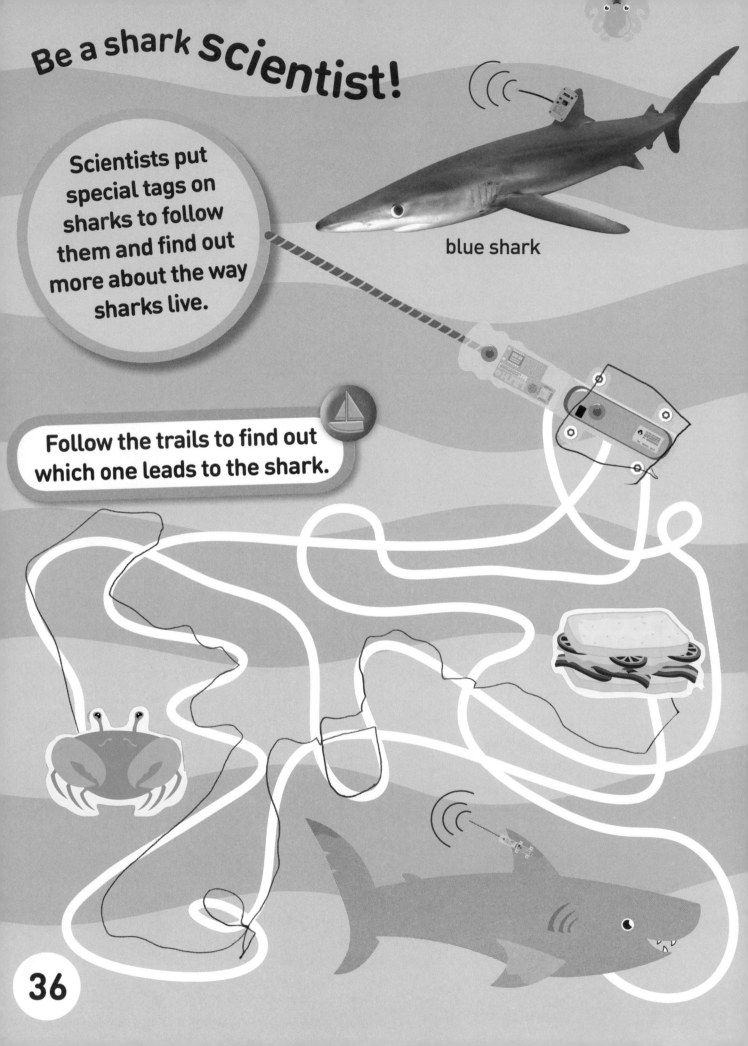

Scientists put special tags on sharks to follow them and find out more about the way sharks live.

blue shark

Follow the trails to find out which one leads to the shark.

Connect the dots to find out who is swimming with the sharks.

Sticker more sharks and divers.

Fin-tastic shark facts!

Bull sharks head-butt their prey!

Hammerhead sharks can find a stingray even when it is hidden under the sand!

Follow the trails to find the stingray!

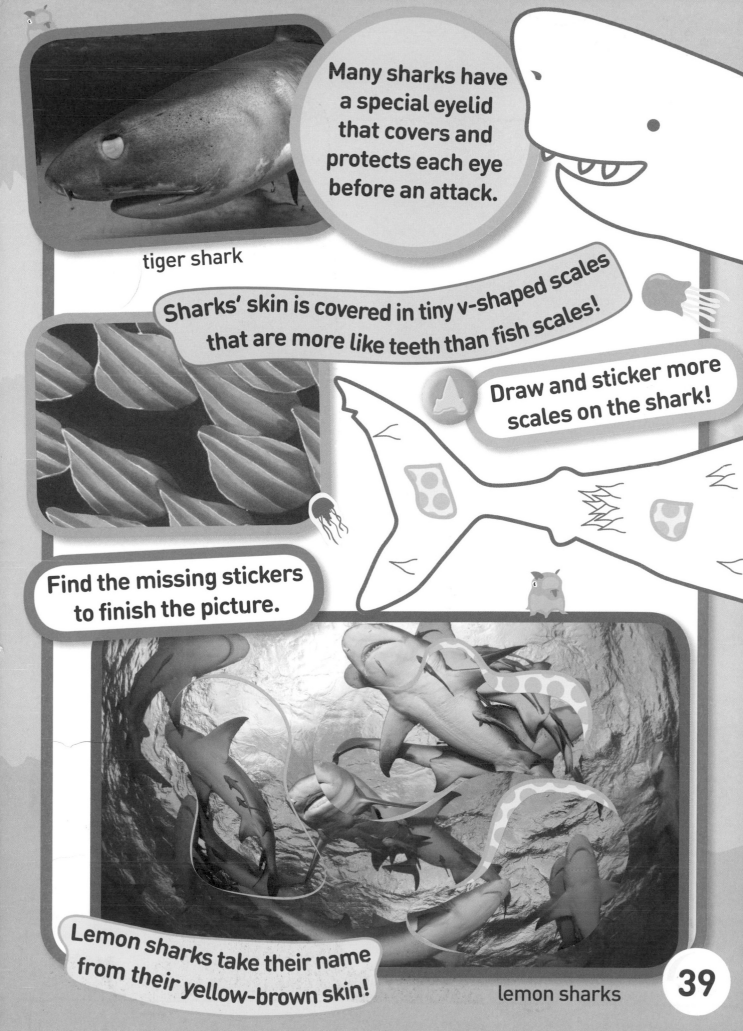

Many sharks have a special eyelid that covers and protects each eye before an attack.

tiger shark

Sharks' skin is covered in tiny v-shaped scales that are more like teeth than fish scales!

Draw and sticker more scales on the shark!

Find the missing stickers to finish the picture.

Lemon sharks take their name from their yellow-brown skin!

lemon sharks

My favorite sharks!

Color and sticker the shark friends!

whitetip reef shark

nurse shark

Draw yourself swimming with sharks!

Who's hiding in the cave?

great white shark